R. VAUGHAN WILLIAMS

BURLEY HEATH

EDITED BY

JAMES FRANCIS BROWN

STUDY SCORE

MUSIC DEPARTMENT

OXFORD
UNIVERSITY PRESS

OXFORD
UNIVERSITY PRESS

Great Clarendon Street, Oxford OX2 6DP,
United Kingdom

Oxford University Press is a department of the University of Oxford.
It furthers the University's objective of excellence in research, scholarship,
and education by publishing worldwide. Oxford is a registered trade mark of
Oxford University Press in the UK and in certain other countries

First published 2013

Impression: 1

ISBN 978–0–19–339939–6 (study score)
ISBN 978–0–19–339547–3 (on hire)

Music origination by Enigma Music Production Services, Amersham, Bucks.

Printed in Great Britain on acid-free paper by
Caligraving Ltd, Thetford, Norfolk

CONTENTS

PREFACE

In the final decade of the nineteenth century Vaughan Williams was preoccupied with the models of the more recent, European attitudes to symphonic thinking; Brahms, Wagner, Liszt, and Richard Strauss figured prominently in the English composer's understanding of structural cohesion, and their personal idioms naturally left their mark on the young composer. Now, however, it was becoming clear to him that he should attempt to detach himself from the dominance of such influences, but it was not until his studies with Ravel in 1907–08 that he began to feel a true resolution to the impasse.

By 1902 there was already a change of emphasis in the composer's thinking; a study of Charles Stanford's *Irish Rhapsody No. 1* (published in 1902) may have encouraged Vaughan Williams to consider a more programmatic approach, serving to loosen some formal constraints and allow a heightened sense of 'flavour' to permeate the music. From this period his interest in folksong is increasingly perceptible in the use, for example, of melodies derived from modal and pentatonic scales. He also experienced a burgeoning interest in reflective romantic poetry and a concern to discover not only his own artistic voice but an authentic Englishness that he considered to be essential for the musical well-being of the nation. These matters were the subject of considerable discussion and correspondence with, among others, Gustav Holst, and this period also marks the beginning of the famous walking tours with that composer.

It was therefore natural that Vaughan Williams should seek inspiration in the English countryside (in this case, one may call it Hardy's 'Wessex') and, in particular, the regions that he was able to explore on foot or bicycle in the company of his friends and family. In late 1902 the composer began a suite of *Four Impressions for Orchestra* to be called *In the New Forest*. *Burley Heath* was to be the first movement, but this and the second 'impression', *The Solent*, are the only works to survive from the four. In fact, although *Burley Heath* was probably complete in conception (as will be discussed), it was not fully written-out and was therefore not performed during the composer's lifetime.

Despite his endeavours, during this period, to achieve stylistic independence through the use of picturesque, geographical titles and a rather more rhapsodic sense of form, *Burley Heath* still reveals the influence of the Germanic approach. This may be discerned, for instance, in the sequence of pithy developmental fragments (bars 40–66). There are also echoes of Strauss's *Don Juan*, perhaps, in the leaping figure at bars 26–32. The trio section (beginning at bar 105) has the sunny appeal and rhythmic lift of Dvořák, coupled with that composer's penchant for the subdominant and the delightful use of pizzicato. Yet, even here, we can discern the musical personality of Vaughan Williams. The use of pentatonic scales (for instance, bars 107–9), also familiar to Dvořák from his encounters with negro spirituals, demonstrates that Vaughan Williams was not so much in the habit of eschewing influences as somehow, charmingly, making them his own.

The completion of the score

Burley Heath has long been thought incomplete—abandoned, after 173 bars, in favour, perhaps, of work on *The Solent*. However, study of the manuscript reveals that the missing material pertains to the recapitulation of a work in ternary form and that the repeated material is intentionally abridged. A comparison of bars 170–3 with bars 79–82 shows that the home tonality of G has been attained and that copying out the repeat of the coda would have been purely procedural. It remained only for the editor to restate the minor key in the viola (bars 193–5) and provide the final three bars. Here, the use of bare pizzicato in cellos and basses is derived from bar 16.

It cannot, of course, be proved that the composer would not have provided another episode at this point, but the tonal balance suggests otherwise. The work's peroration appears to come in the passage from bar 135 to bar 142 of the trio, and the short recapitulation therefore conveys an ominous sense of dissolution—a returning to the shadows whence the music came.

JAMES FRANCIS BROWN
July 2013

MANUSCRIPT AND TEXTUAL NOTES

The full-score manuscript is bound in a single volume together with the manuscripts of *The Solent* and *Harnham Down* in the music collection of the British Library (Add. MS 57278). The title page bears the inscription: *New Forest* [in blue pencil] then: *In the New Forest | Four Impressions for Orchestra | by R. Vaughan Williams | I. Burley Heath.*

At the bottom of the title page, there is a handwritten note: *Withdrawn by the composer who intended to destroy the MS. Therefore not for performance, Ursula Vaughan Williams.*

On the reverse of the title page is an instrumentation list that is reproduced here for the interesting references to the other intended works:

Instruments Employed | Woodwind—2 flutes, 1 oboe, 1 cor anglais (2nd oboe in IV), 2 clarinets, 2 bassoons | Brass—4 horns in F, 2 trumpets in F, 3 trombones, 1 bass tuba | (horns III & IV are silent in no. II trumpets are silent in no. II | trombones and tuba are silent on nos. I & II.) | Percussion—timpani, triangle. | (Timpani are silent in no II. triangle is silent in I, II and IV) | Strings —1st violins, 2nd violins, violas, violoncelli and double basses.)

It is interesting to note that the brass instruments marked as 'silent' in movement II are in fact used in *The Solent*. This may indicate that the order of movements was not determined from the outset.

There are several deletions made by scratching out with a blade, but no reordering or pasting of material. There are several blank pages throughout the score that do not affect the continuity and presumably result from convenience in working with the manuscript paper. Many notational inconsistencies deemed to be mistakes have been discreetly amended for uniformity, but where doubt arises square brackets have been used.

On page two of the manuscript (after bar 16 in the published score) there is a single instance of blue pencil marking, perhaps indicating performance preparation, subsequently abandoned.

This edition follows the composer's method of indicating phrase marks rather than bowing, which accounts for several instances of repeated notes within slurs in the strings.

The trumpet parts in the manuscript are for instruments in F and have here been transcribed for trumpets in B♭.

Rehearsal numbers are not given in the manuscript and have been supplied by the editor.

There is no initial tempo indication or metronome mark in the manuscript. These have been supplied by the editor.

11	The figure in the cor anglais is mostly notated with a slur over two bars. There are some instances of the figure with an internal slur over the first two staccato notes, but the former notation has been adopted here.
70	MS—the bar following this is deleted.
120	MS—Two blank pages follow.
141	MS—Two blank pages follow.

ORCHESTRATION

2 Flutes

Oboe

Cor Anglais

2 Clarinets

2 Bassoons

4 Horns (in F)

2 Trumpets (in B♭)

Timpani

Strings

Duration: *c*.6 minutes

Study scores of *Harnham Down* (978–0–19–339940–2) and *The Solent* (978–0–19–339941–9) are also available on sale, and complete orchestral material is available on hire/rental.

Burley Heath

R. VAUGHAN WILLIAMS

Printed in Great Britain

OXFORD UNIVERSITY PRESS, MUSIC DEPARTMENT, GREAT CLARENDON STREET, OXFORD OX2 6DP

12

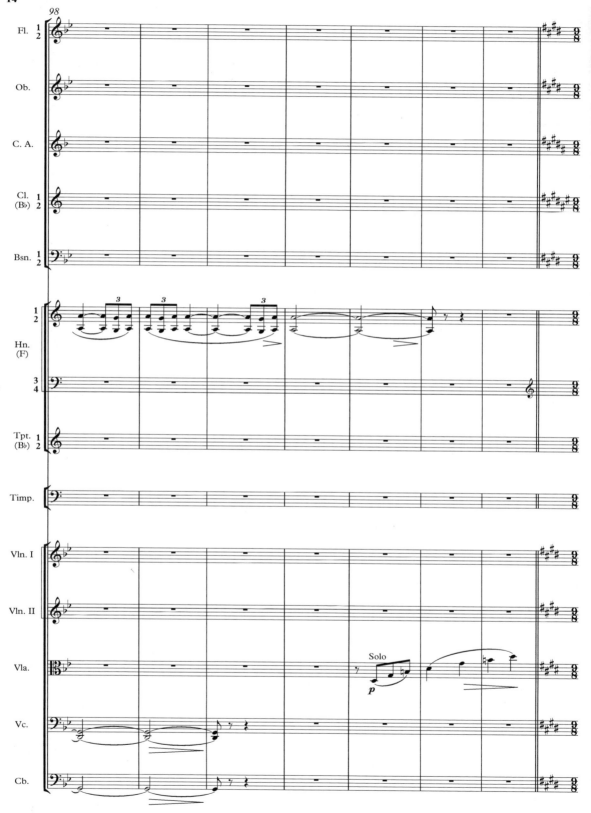

allargando

189
Fl. 1 2
Ob.
C. A.
Cl. (B♭) 1 2
Bsn. 1 2
Hn. (F) 1 2 3 4
Tpt. (B♭) 1 2
Timp.
Vln. I
Vln. II
Vla.
Solo
p
ppp
Vc.
Tutti, pizz.
pp dim.
ppp
Cb.
pizz.
pp dim.
ppp